A Culture of Governance

The design and implementation of a governance program is a challenging thing to undertake. It is more than difficult to gain full business user acceptance. Governance seems very invasive to the business data owners and stewards. A tension exists between IT Data Services and business operations that threatens the adoption and longevity of the program.

Transformation must occur within the organization. Data governance must take root and grow into full Information Governance. Governance operations must broaden to include unstructured business data sources and the context that the business brings to interlaced data concepts.

This transformation is possible. Using the GOVERN method, Templar provides a roadmap for the governance program to become part of the culture of the organization.

By following these six principles you can GOVERN to greatness:

- G = Grow the Program
- O= Optimize and Operationalize
- V = Value the Program
- E = Evolve the Program
- R = Revisit Core Principles
- N = Neutralize Naysayers

Building on the foundation set in her first book, *get Governed: Building World Class Data Governance Programs*, Templar guides you through the process needed to meld governance into operations to create a Culture of Governance.

A *Culture* of Governance

Morgan Templar

Ivory Lady Publishing
Rescue, California

Copyright

Published in the United States of America by
Ivory Lady Publishing; Rescue, California

Printed in the United States of America

First Edition, 2018

ISBN 10: 0692185100

ISBN 13: 978-0692185100

Cover Design by Stephen Templar

Author's photo courtesy of Stephen Templar

Information Governance vs. Data Governance courtesy of the Information Coalition. Used with Permission.

A *Culture* of Governance

All my Best!
-Morgan Templar

Dedication

For the many Information and Data Governance professionals who share their knowledge, experience and practices in the pursuit of excellence in governance!

It takes a special kind of dedication to keep pushing the stone uphill. May this help smooth your path as you strive to create a culture of governance.

Foreword

Expertise on data and information governance experts is pretty rare. Even more rare are experts who can explain it to the rest of us.

I first met Morgan Templar after reading her first book, *get Governed*. That book impressed me with its clear and straightforward explanation of how to build a governance program, from strategy to implementation to measurement, in any organization. Since then, *get Governed* has been my "go to" when asked by customers and clients for a practical guide for building a governance program.

Meeting Morgan in person was like having the narrator of her book come alive. Here was a person with deep expertise in a sometimes-arcane field, but with the ability to explain complex concepts clearly and simply and using great examples and stories from her direct experience. And with verve and a dash of humor as well.

Since then, Morgan and I have collaborated on a number of projects and initiatives. We work well together because we share a common perspective on data and information governance, which is that "it does not have to be that hard".

What we call data and information governance has its roots in records management, and records management in turn is a discipline related to library sciences. And it is all built upon a foundation of paper.

Concepts of "declaring" records and defining retention rules are based on a time when we put paper records in boxes, marked a date on the box and put it in the basement. We defined a role called records manager, and we told them that it is their job to figure out what to keep, how to categorize it and when to get rid of it.

That foundation is not robust enough for managing the vast amounts of digital information we are accumulating in business now. The statistics are staggering – one commonly-cited metric is that over the last two years alone 90 percent of the data in the world was generated. And every minute, 156 million email messages are sent. So, we need new tools and new methods for managing the information we are creating within our organizations.

And managing that information is critical. Over-retention of data wastes money, of course, but more importantly it creates unacceptable risk. More stored information means a larger surface area for data theft and more risk of being out of compliance with regulatory requirements, two risks that, if unmanaged, can result in an organization being on the front page of the Wall Street Journal for failing to protect its customers data.

The good news is that, while technology got us into this, technology is providing new tools to get us out of it. With automatic classification capabilities built on artificial intelligence methods and the ability to analyze huge volumes of information with "big data" techniques, we have the capability to create data and information governance programs on a new technology foundation, beyond boxed and barcodes.

The challenge of gaining support and compliance, of course, remains. We have the tools, now we need the commitment of the organization. And that is why Morgan's new book, *A Culture of Governance*, has such an important role to play.

Morgan and I share a passion for simplifying data and information governance concepts, making them easy to understand and easy to apply. I focus more on the technology; Morgan is focused on the people and the program.

In *A Culture of Governance*, Morgan provides an easy-to-follow program for embedding the thinking and processes of governance within the fabric of an organization. That means that good data and information governance is not "another" thing we have to ask employees to do, it is instead embedded in their everyday behavior. And that is a critical shift in moving our organizations forward toward a "future state" where all information is categorized, managed, retained and destroyed on a systematically, automatic and predictable basis.

I am jealous as you move on to the first chapter of *A Culture of Governance.* You will find clearly communicated, practical advice for building a culture of governance in your own organization.

Ken Lownie
Vice President, North American Sales
EverTeam, Inc.
Boston – Paris – Lyon - Bangalore

Table of Contents

Chapter 1 – Introduction

"Innovation comes out of great human ingenuity and very personal passions." – Megan Smith

Data and Information Governance are still very much in their infancy. The existence of programs has been steadily growing over the past 15 years. But most companies are struggling to develop programs that can catch up with the lightspeed change of technology. The foundations of how business gets done are being challenged and changed every day. Ephemeral communication, privacy, encryption, and blockchain are just a few of the disrupters. They are changing the way we do business, how we think about information, and are quickly becoming part of our corporate cultures. Litigation and privacy challenges are only beginning to occur leaving us with few hard and fast rules to follow. The methods of governing these new technologies are still immature.

Do you have a program established but can't seem to find the expected return on investment (ROI)? Did your software vendor promise to help you establish a governance program as part of the implementation but stopped at data classification? Do your business users know how to be information stewards? Do they even know your governance program exists?

These questions are being asked all over the world. The introduction of the General Data Protection Regulation (GDPR) in Europe and the passing of a similar bills in California and New York in 2018 and the pending bills in several other states in the USA have highlighted not only the need and desire of consumers to see their data protected but a significant gap in the structures to support privacy and governance.

It isn't enough to relegate data and information governance to the provenance of legal discovery in the eventuality of when, not if, your company is sued or fined by a consumer group or regulatory body. The risk to organizations is simply too great and growing every day.

But how do you change all of this? In one single word – Culture. A Culture of Governance is required to put the full might of your organization toward protecting and governing your most precious asset – Information.

When every employee literally has your network in their pocket; when crucial decisions and discussions about your business are made with text messaging and apps like Slack; when consumers are clamoring for their information to be protected and the right to be forgotten – This is the moment that you need every leader, every employee, every 3rd party vendor to appreciate the precariousness of the situation and to be a part of your foundation for strong protection of information balanced by access and availability for data driven decisions. This is the time that your information governance program needs to become A Culture of Governance.

Chapter 2 – A brief history of Information Governance

"The only way you survive is you continuously transform into something else. It's this idea of continuous transformation that makes you an innovation company."
– Ginni Rometty

Information governance began within the information technology (IT) organizations of many companies. It started as Information Security (IS) and, through pressure from regulatory bodies, grew into the monitoring of business activities through Internal Audit organizations (IA).

IT has the accountability to ensure system integrity. They are accountable to ensure that integrations function properly. Enterprise, Information, System, and Data Architects develop data models and data dictionaries, data classification systems, integration mapping, city-scape models of capabilities, systems, and reference architecture. All of this is critical to keep systems running and minimize technology failures.

IS monitors password protocols and access to systems. They train users on cybersecurity, phishing techniques, and avoiding data breaches. Their primary function is to keep a corral around the information owned, managed, and/or used by the company to ensure that it does not fall into the wrong hands. In some companies, they are accountable for compliance with applicable Privacy regulations. They are often the group that grants access to systems, shared drives, and file structures. The Help Desk and Training arms of IT sometimes fall under IS; at the very least they are a critical component of those functions.

IA has the accountability to ensure that privacy and regulatory requirements are met by business users. They monitor business user access to systems. They ensure separation of duties between people who can modify critical information, such as banking data, and people who can utilize that information in order to prevent fraud. They audit information management by business users, process map documents, data dissemination, and assure the proper use of information to protect the company from regulatory audit findings and fines.

The Business is the part of each organization that understands, collects, enters, and uses the information in these technology systems – they provide the Context for the Content. They may have private data stores and Access databases on their personal machines or shared drives. They may have entire business intelligence and reporting organizations. Often the Business will go so far as to create "shadow IT" organizations to fulfill their appetite and need for information in a faster, more dynamic, but less controlled manner.

These four groups, IT, IS, IA, and the Business are extant in almost every company these days. So, why does anyone need another layer?

Think of these organizations like a cake. It seems very solid and organized.

What happens when technology or your industry changes?

What will hold the layers together?

What will keep the middle layers from sliding away from the top and bottom layers?

What if we could apply some kind of glue to hold them all together?

Well, we have. It is called Information and Data Governance.

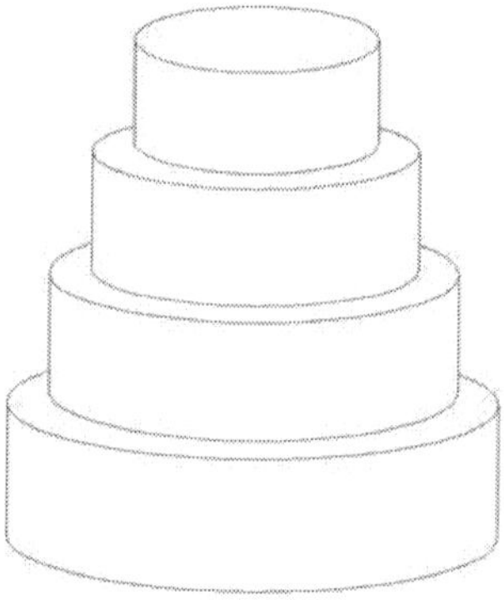

Information and Data Governance, when implemented well, permeates all layers of a company. It is directed by the most senior leaders of the organization to keep its outcomes in line with Strategic Goals and Objectives. Information is "owned" by the Business. Data is "managed" by IT. Stewards come from the Business with their understanding of the content and context of data as information. IS and IA monitor the data use and management processes and technical systems to ensure that decisions fall within acceptable standards and regulations.

In short, Governance becomes the frosting that glues each layer together and covers the outside to protect the interior structure.

A quick note here – generally when using the term "Information Governance" we are referring to the activities of the Business and IA, and when we use the term "Data Governance" we are referring to the activities of IT and IS. However, the terms are used almost interchangeably in literature and at conferences. I generally stick to using the term "Governance" regardless of Business or IT, just for simplification. There are purists who insist on one or the other; I'm not one of those. I believe you should use the terminology that resonates with your company vernacular or industry.

I have worked in Information and Data Governance my entire career. Long before the terms were coined, we had data management or service organizations. For most of my career I have worked in "the Business" but I have always found myself in the role of translator between business and IT. I grew up "speaking tech" at home and have a strong technical background.

These days I am focused on expanding the profession of Governance. I believe strongly in the utilization of Governance as a method to unite non-technical business information experts with technical data scientists, analysts and architects.

The Governance organization is the binding agent that will enable impending technological advancements. Very important decisions will be made in very near future about the context and content of information available to Artificial Intelligence (AI) and machine learning algorithms. These are complicated technical decisions that must be based on Business understanding and usage. The Governance organization provides a framework for that collaboration.

Some of you are thinking, "How do I go about setting up a Governance program?" I provide a step-by-step 'How To' in my first book, *get Governed: Building World Class Data Governance Programs.*

(©Morgan Templar 2017 published by Ivory Lady Publishing) I have made some of these resources available publicly on my website, www.getgoverned.com.

But you may be thinking, "We have a governance program. But it's limited in scope and/or somewhat dysfunctional." If that's you, this book provides a framework to optimize and improve your governance program. By following the GOVERN method, you will find a path to turn your governance program into a valued asset. These six steps will help you justify the program you have now and generate renewed excitement for cementing governance into your company culture.

GOVERN stands for:

- G = Grow the Program
- O= Optimize and Operationalize
- V = Value the Program
- E = Evolve the Program
- R = Revisit Core Principles
- N = Neutralize Naysayers

Chapter 3 – G = Grow the Program

"Exploration is the engine that drives innovation. Innovation drives economic growth. So, let's all go exploring." – Edith Widder

Most Governance programs are established in conjunction with or adjacent to the implementation of a Data Lake (DL) or Enterprise Data Warehouse (EDW). It is a prime opportunity since the data mapping and classification efforts must be completed as part of these massive technical projects and the Business subject matter experts (SME's) must participate for success.

Typical components of one of these types of programs include a Master Data Management tool and stewards, a data dictionary of the information in the DL or EDW, some level of effort to engage the business in defining the terms for a standardized glossary, an information quality program and a data model of the DL or EDW.

Some programs have gone so far as to establish specific data domains and data/information stewards and may even have a Governance Steering Committee, Data Owner's Council or Governance Steward's Council.

A very few companies, relatively speaking, have Chief Data Officers or Vice President of Analytics, Governance and Privacy, or some similar title. Even more uncommon is a complementary "business" role that is a senior leader who champions business adoption and participation in governance.

Companies that have invested in such leadership roles typically have some investment in full-time staff that act as steward liaisons between the Business and the Governance Steering Committee/ Data Owner's Council. Or they may have reclassified certain roles and individuals to fall within their organizations.

Most Governance programs fall under the purview of the Chief Information Officer, even in cases where an additional C-suite or VP role has been created. This alignment with the IT/IS organization makes sense during the initial implementation of a program, especially when established, as mentioned above, as part of a large IT initiative. But at some point, the Business must be granted a voice and leadership to mature and grow the program.

The long-term prognosis of successful Governance programs relies heavily on continued support of the CIO. No amount of Business prodding has enough weight to overcome the generally solid and planned roadmap of the IT organization. Governance must be grown as a joint IT/Business strategic objective handed down from the senior leaders of an organization.

Rather than devote a large amount of time and space in this book reviewing the many potential trouble-spots you may be facing, I recommend taking a look at the white paper entitled, "Common Trouble Spots When Implementing Data Governance," found on page 195 of *get Governed* or on my website, https://www.getgoverned.com/common-trouble-spots. But, let's get back to ways to grow your program.

Case study after case study has shown that regardless of the maturity of your program there are opportunities for growth in three areas:

1. Expand Governance to New Data Domains, Data Sets, or Processes
2. Govern new or additional Systems (which might include unstructured data)
3. Streamline and consolidate Functions through Governance

Expand to New Data Domains, Data Sets or Processes

The first step is to identify what data and information you are already governing. This is an excellent opportunity to sit down with an Enterprise Information or Data Architect and compare your program to their system and process city scape. You will find areas that are not currently covered under your initial program.

Make a list of these processes and identify which Data Owner is accountable for the team or department. If you can classify every known process under a specific Owner, your work just got very easy. If not, you will need to go through the process of establishing a New Data Owner and starting the education process in greater detail.

Existing Data Owners

When the non-governed process or data-set is identified as belonging to an existing Data Owner, follow this process:

- Prepare the list and meet with the Data Owner
- Get their feedback on the importance of the process or information
- Create a prioritized list that includes any Key Performance Indicators (KPIs) that are being reported on this information
- Work with the Data Owner to begin to apply governance to those process areas

It is important to note that if information is already being measured and reported on as a Metric or KPI, then it should be under the care of the Governance organization.

Be aware that expanding Governance to new processes or teams under an existing Data Owner will require time, effort, and potentially additional business resources. Sometimes those resources are trainers and change management experts who will step in and teach the business SME's about how to Govern their data. Sometimes the needed resources are business SME's who may be taking on additional duties to measure data quality or manage the governance process. Your specific governance organization, the amount of inherent bureaucracy in the company, and the scope of the growth will all be factors in the number of resources and the depth of their involvement in the expansion.

Be aware that there may be perfectly legitimate reasons that a process or data set is not governed. And while it is the responsibility of the Data Owner to determine the right fit for inclusion, you should expect some resistance. Human nature naturally resists change. Fear of change, resistance to new demands on employee's time, or other valid reasons may be brought up as reasons to delay inclusion in the governance process.

The honest truth is that not all information needs to be governed, today. But all information repositories and sources should be identified and evaluated before making that determination. In a future state of AI driven data processes, every bit and byte of data will have to be governed to some extent. But today, with people in the mix, we can rely on well-trained individuals to make appropriate decisions about the care and use of information assets. Just be aware that efforts to automate processes relay on the appropriate classification, definition, and context of information to succeed.

New Data Domains with New Data Owners

When data sets or processes are identified in the review with Enterprise Information Architecture as not currently governed and the logical owner of that information or process is not currently part of your governance organization as a Data Owner, the process has a few additional steps.

1. Challenge your assumption that the information needs governance.
   a. Why was it left out of the initial IT project scope?
   b. Is it in a future DL or EDW project phase?
   c. Was it missed?
   d. Is it measured in a KPI?
   e. Is it critical for regulatory, security, or audit compliance?
   f. Apply your standards for governance consistently across all domains.
2. Once it is determined that the information or process should be governed, begin with the Data Owner
   a. Ensure that you have executive level support for naming a new data owner. This may need to go through the Executive Steering Committee.

b. Find a mentor who is already a Data Owner and jointly present the role and responsibilities to the new Data Owner.
c. Be sure that you include the right amount of training materials and resources. But don't rely only on written material. A mentor to help guide and encourage is critical to long-term sustainability (this is true at all levels of program maturity and organization hierarchy).

3. Show up prepared with a model or framework for governance but be ready to engage in negotiations with the new data owner about your assumptions around the data or process.
4. Once the new Data Owner is on board the process begins to resemble the method described above when expanding within an existing data domain.

Govern new or additional Systems

- which might include unstructured data or information

The two most common places for Governance to be missed are in Middleware and Unstructured Data.

Middleware

Middleware encompasses all the systems that exist between the primary business systems in an architectural stack. This might include a system that translates information from the language of one system to another or a message broker type of system which enables a publish/subscribe function between systems. It might be a system that meters that transference of data to ensure that the sending system doesn't overwhelm the capacity of the receiving system intake. Or a system that creates batch jobs for ETL (Extract/Transform/Load) integrations. It may be a security monitoring system or protocol.

For the most part, middleware is the domain of IT. System monitoring and protocols should be implemented to ensure that data is properly flowing from system to system enabling information access and use by the appropriate business team.

Governance of middleware goes beyond ensuring that the data between systems is flowing. It requires some business engagement to ensure that no context is lost and that the monitoring systems are set up properly to begin with. Let me give you an example of good governance of a middleware system that included the business as a key participant.

Jake managed a provider enrollment team at a healthcare insurance company. His team was responsible to load information into a provider data management system that integrated into a claims payment system. The performance of Jake's team was measured against many KPI's, since this is a critical component of health insurance operations.

Because errors were usually identified in the downstream claims system, Jake, a data steward for the Provider domain, had his team monitor not only the creation and management of data (business processes) but the successful arrival of that data downstream in the claims system (technical integration). This monitoring included more than context audits. They worked with IT application development and built a system that both sent a daily report of the number of records modified in the provider data management system AND by integration into the downstream claims system via integration. It also allowed them to actively look at the integration and translation functions in real time. While the number of transmitted records from the management system arriving at the claims system never exactly matched due to system record structural differences, they had developed a working ratio that ensured the smooth transference of information from one system to the next. They also had a system in place to manually resolve records that "fell out*" of integration between these transactional systems because of some kind of error. (*Record was not able to be processed by the integration and information had to manually loaded to one or both systems to ensure successful data cohesion.)

Setting up this kind of joint monitoring between the IT database administrators and the Business data steward had been a very long process (about 18 months) of development and collaboration.

One day the business analyst who monitored the integrations came to Jake's office. "We're missing half of the messages that should have been sent to the claims system last weekend. It looks like it may have been happening for at least three days." Those were not the words Jake wanted to hear. This meant that potentially thousands of claims were either processed or payed incorrectly due to missing key information.

Jake quickly got on the phone with the Product Owners of both transactional systems and the IT Data Custodian. They called an emergency troubleshooting meeting that included representatives managing each of the potential failure points. After several hours of tracing the data flow it was determined that one of the two servers that processed message broker had overloaded and the error message logged in the middle of the night on server two was missed by the database administrator. Half of the data, the half on server one, the functional server, was getting through. And because data was being sent and received by both transactional systems, no priority alert was fired. Upon closer examination it was found that a single batch job had been loaded onto server two which had overloaded it. It had stopped translating and passing information.

Several team's work and information loaded into a handful of transactional systems were supposed to be flowing via this server. Jake's proactive monitoring activities and collaboration with IT identified and helped resolve the issue before it became an irreparable situation.

Do your business data stewards have this kind of visibility? Jake's team did have a custom monitoring system built and is more involved in the management and stewardship of their information than most. But regardless of the method, the key message is that successful transmission and receipt of information from system to system is a shared accountability of both IT and Business. When KPIs are properly established that include information being available across systems, there is justification and urgency for the business to be involved in the process and for IT to become more transparent.

System integrations and middleware are an ideal place to look for places to better govern data and information. Take a look at the following drawing. What is often represented as a single "integration" may actually be a complex set of automated processes and activities occurring in the middleware.

Figure 1: Simplified middleware ETL diagram

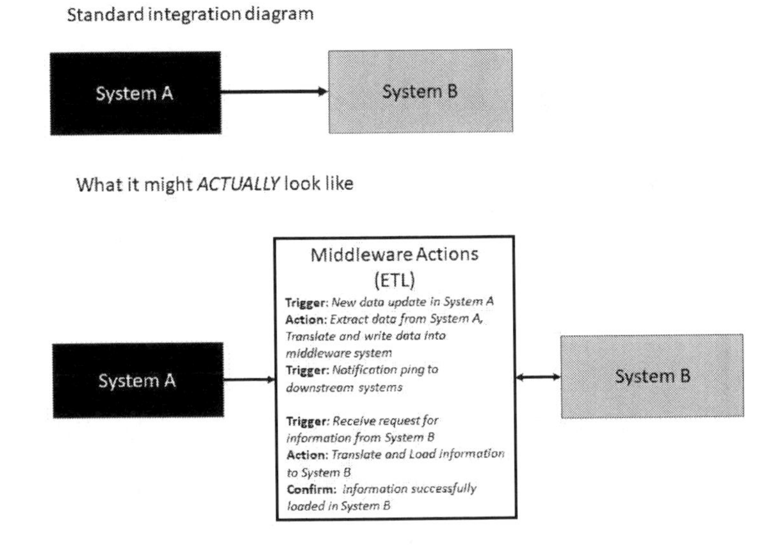

This example is highly simplified, as most middleware transactions involve several systems and processes. But it is intended to provide a nudge. What is sitting between your transactional systems? Who is accountable for the accuracy, context, quantity, performance, and speed of the integration? Clearly the information and processes should fall under formal governance. Is this policy, process, or system?

Middleware is the place where the most complex "data errors" can occur because of the language translations that occur during an ETL process. It's relatively easy to identify if a person mistyped something and put in 2301 instead of 2013. But the sometimes subtle, and sometimes massive, changes that must occur to move information from one system to another can cause issues that are often not identified or understood until information has moved many steps along the lifecycle.

Here's a funny example of how translations can get mixed up: the 1975 movie, "Monty Python and the Holy Grail." The title in Japanese is "Monty Python

Seihei." Now translate it back to English: "Monty Python and the Sacred Sake Cup." It loses quite a bit of context, although it is technically correct. A Data Steward may argue that "Sacred Sake Cup" is accurate. An Information Steward would understand that "technically correct" and "contextually correct" are not the same thing. This example illustrates that business context must be a component of middleware development and ongoing accuracy.

Unstructured Data

Unstructured Data is, without any question, the most hotly contested kind of information when talking about a Governance Program. Let's start with a definition. I should note here that there are as many definitions of "unstructured data" as there are companies or associations. I'm going with a middle-of-the-line definition from the mighty Wikipedia.

> *"Unstructured data or information is information that either does not have a pre-defined data model or is not organized a pre-defined manner. Unstructured information is typically text-heavy,*

but may contain data such as dates, numbers and facts, as well. This results in irregularities and ambiguities that make it difficult to understand using traditional programs as compared to data stored in field form in databases or annotated (semantically tagged) in documents." *

*Wikipedia contributors. (2018, October 8). Unstructured data. In *Wikipedia, The Free Encyclopedia*. Retrieved August 8, 2018, from https://en.wikipedia.org/w/index.php?title=Unstructured_data&oldid=863073233

Unstructured data, then, can be any information that is not in a **predefined** format. This could include Access databases (more on this later), email, text messages, recorded video conferences, Word documents, scans and images, and the list can go on and on.

It is a general assumption that Information Technology (IT) will *only* manage structured data – information that can be classified, defined, captured in a predefined structured manner, and is easily machine readable. I have personally been told by an IT Vice President, "Data belongs to IT and

Information belongs to the Business." Okay, so that is one way of saying that the Business provides context. BUT, is the person at the head of IT a Chief DATA Officer? Or is she a Chief INFORMATION Officer? When a hacker gets into the network and downloads 200,000 patient medical records which includes 'classification' by Social Security Number, and 'column headings' including name, address, and Date of Birth ... will the headline in the Los Angeles Times be about the head of "Business" or will it be about the CIO?

ALL information requires some kind of Governance. And all Governance needs joint activities between Business and IT.

Most of the work done by Business teams is in unstructured formats. Faxes come in from doctors and may be paper or imaged. Telephone calls are fielded by Customer Service. Business analysts download reports of the data their team manages and places it in Access databases to identify trends, to better respond to requests for information, or to interact with other teams or third parties. The entire company uses email, instant messenger, and texts and many critical decisions are made via this "written" communication. Crucial decisions are made during conversations on recorded or unrecorded video or teleconferences that might be "discoverable" in a lawsuit.

Is the answer to encrypt everything? Is the answer to lock down access to information to only IT? These are methods of creating an illusion of security. Since IT doesn't know the context, how can they steward that information?

The answer is to include this information in your Governance Program and ensure that the Business participates.

The best methods of governance include policies for each of these kinds of unstructured data and ephemeral communication. These policies should include:

- The content that is appropriate or inappropriate for the medium

- A method of review and access to the information
- The method and security of storage
- The retention periods
- Methods of archiving
- Reference to the specific Regulation or Standard that has guided the policy
- Author, Date and Approver Names for the policy

In a perfect world every business or IT process, business or IT policy, and Governance decision should be referenceable to either a Regulation, Accreditation Standard, Legal Agreement or Contract, Company Policy, or Industry Benchmark. It is the role of the Governance Organization to ensure the compliance of everyone in the company either through an existing structure (tech support ticketing, internal audit, etc.) or through policy overseen by the governance or business group.

The logistics of this type of governance also fall under the purview of the Governance Organization. And guidelines should include regular review and update. Most audits by regulatory or accreditation groups are checking to see if you are following your own policies first and then if your policy adequately fulfills the standard. Policies that are outdated, not followed, duplicates, or contradictory are where companies get into trouble. And while it was once a common practice to intentionally choose not to implement governance and respond with an apology, recent, very public cases, have shown that the consequences of governance negligence may be severely punitive, and an apology is only the first step in a settlement.

If information is used, captured, or stored that cannot be referenced to one of the above guides, it must be seriously examined to understand why it is captured at all.

Streamline and consolidate Functions through Governance

One of the great benefits of a well-governed organization is a map of the information used, stored, and managed in the company, otherwise known as a Business Data Model.

An Information Glossary is another critical asset. When an information glossary is first established, care must be taken to disallow multiple definitions for a single term or multiple terms with the same definition. These are common methods for one business silo to try to maintain control of information that may be used or created by a different silo.

Simple, rationalized definitions are crucial to eliminate duplicate maintenance or access of information.

When duplicate information maintenance is discovered, examine the "why." Ask these questions:

- Is the transaction in question adding information to a data set or are they making changes?
- Is the same information maintained manually in more than one system by one or more teams?

- Is the same information received from more than one source, and if so, what is the source of truth?

Answering these questions can provide a roadmap for the elimination of administrative overhead. A word of caution here. Teams are likely to be somewhat resistant to the idea of giving control of "their information" to another team. Good change management techniques will come into play here. Ownership and control should be mutually agreed upon and should be as far upstream in an organization as possible.

I have seen entire systems that were duplicates for different lines of business. The same records, the same addresses, the same names, the same everything, except for perhaps small additional details such as participation in a specific program or negotiated payment terms.

Good governance programs will be a platform to discover these kinds of duplication and to facilitate appropriate decisions about the source of truth. You must ask if it is more or less costly to add a field to one system than it is to have one or more teams maintain duplicate information. In some cases, the answer may be yes. But if it is yes, the long-term consequences need to be weighed, including the potential for conflicting information and data storage costs of information in more than one system. It isn't always about the simple people cost of data entry people.

Identifying these pockets of redundancy can justify the cost of the governance program. Sometimes teams can be combined, and sometimes a team can be eliminated, simply by changing one or two fields in a particular system and modifying an integration.

Chapter 3 Summary

The growth of your governance program will follow a maturity cycle. A new program will find countless places where governance offers benefits to both business and IT. A more established program will be working on finessing their scope and processes. Understand where your program is in its maturity cycle. Then take advantage of these opportunities to grow your program:

- Expand Governance to New Data Domains, Data Sets, or Processes
- Govern new or additional Systems (which might include unstructured data)
- Streamline and consolidate Functions through Governance

Growing in a planned and structured manner in conjunction with business and IT leadership will help build the trust of the organization and the relationships needed to collaborate in the short and long term.

Chapter 4 – O = Optimize and Operationalize

"Without continual growth and progress, such words such as improvement, achievement and success have not meaning." – Benjamin Franklin

Closing the gap between the needs and decision drivers of Business and IT is a crucial step to the long-term success and maturity of your governance program. Going through the optimization process will involve ensuring that the program is operationalized. First, let's look at some strategies to Optimize. Then we'll delve deeper into Operationalizing with the Business.

Optimize the Program

There are many ways to tweak and optimize your program. These will vary by organization. But whether your program is new or well established, there are a couple of universal steps to Optimize your program:

1. Identify opportunities to improve your program's functionality
2. Set Key Performance Indicators (KPIs) to measure the adoption and penetration of governance

These activities will require cooperation and participation by all parties. Optimization should become an ongoing activity. Think Wash, Rinse, Repeat.

Identify functional improvements

Every program begins somewhere. Often, governance begins as part of an IT uplift initiative. Assuming that you have some level of governance organization established, you will find that there are rough patches that keep the program from seamless enterprise-wide adoption.

In my book *get Governed* I shared a checklist for program implementation. You can access a copy of this checklist on my website in the toolkit section: https://www.getgoverned.com/success-checklist. These 16 steps are a good starting point to review in your program to identify gaps. Let's review at each step and see how it applies to optimizing your program.

1. Create a Charter

The steps to create a charter are often overlooked. Especially when the program wasn't started with the intent to be run by the business. A governance committee charter *defines the scope and responsibility of the committee and committee members.* A typical charter will include:

- A Statement of Purpose – why the committee was formed
- The Provenance and Authority under which the committee was formed – What Executive gave authority and to whom does the committee ultimately report
- Description of the roles and responsibilities of the members
- Defined schedule of activities
- How the committee will conduct business, i.e. will it use Robert's Rules of Order or some other method
- Definition of "Majority" and division of votes

- This is critical. Some departments or units will subdivide their stewardship and you will end up with an unbalanced roster. One department should not have the ability to override all others. Think about the divisions in the United States Congress with its House of Representatives and Senate bodies. Regardless of the size of the state, the Senate has equal representation (2 representatives from each state). The House of Representatives has size-based representation (This is very complicated to calculate, but it does allow for population-based allocation of votes. It might be something for you to consider – base votes on the number of employees represented or perhaps on the number of governed systems, etc.) Both methods of allocating votes are valuable, but it is cumbersome to try to replicate this type of model for corporate governance.

    - I generally recommend that each department gets only 1 or 2 votes (you decide) and their votes need to be representative of the majority of votes of the stewards who represent their department.
- A method to elect a Chairperson and the term of office. Also include any other officers that are needed, such as a Communications Chair to take minutes and distribute messaging or a Vice-Chair who will be the next in line to be the Chairperson.
- Sub-committee definitions including how to form and disband these committees
- Scope of authority over operations, projects, or strategic decisions, including a method for these processes to engage the governance council, a process for consideration, and a method to render decisions or opinions
- Schedule to review the charter and methods to make modifications.

Once the charter is written and ratified by the committee, it should be submitted to the Steering

Council and Executive Committee for approval. Your organization may also have a Board of Directors. If so, the Governance Council charter should be submitted to them for review and input.

2. Get Sponsorship from Business leaders

On first glance, this seems like a no-brainer - of course, the business needs to support the governance process. But here is the big disconnect: Governance activities take TIME and business resources are stretched thin. Unless you have real support from business leaders, their people will participate in lackluster ways and your program will not become part of the culture.

Getting business leadership on board is more than a verbal commitment. They need to understand and agree to allow their team members the time, budget and space to participate in meetings, broaden their governance knowledge and contribution potential by attending training (internal or external), and take on additional responsibilities that become a part of their job descriptions.

When you approach a business leader and have an expectation of commitment that flows through their entire structure, right down to rewriting those job descriptions and modifying annual evaluations, they will be hesitant. What seems like a great idea on the surface begins to erode as the required work is understood. Make it as easy as possible for them:

- Provide sample language to include in job descriptions that may need to be modified that is aligned with your program outcomes. In other words, tell them what you want their people to do to support the program.
- Suggest metrics to measure their people against that align with the program metrics. (More about this in the next section.)
- Ensure that the initial buy-in and messaging comes from the top. Your Executive Sponsor should open those doors first.
- Both Business Leaders and Business Stewards should have governance objectives in their annual goals and evaluations. Remember that what gets measured gets done!

You may have already started your program with some level of business support. That's awesome! You still have the opportunity to expand in this area. Each year goals and objectives are revisited. Take the opportunity in early 4th quarter to meet with the business leaders, individually or as a group, to realign your expectations of them and their team.

Give leaders the opportunity to provide constructive criticism and input into how the program is working or how it is affecting their operation. Be flexible, open, and willing to make modifications, if necessary, to make the program work better for everyone.

Above all, recognize that governance is a collaborative venture. You need the business and they need you to make it work. But bottom-up approaches won't work in this instance. You really do need the support of senior leaders before business stewards and analysts will give you their time.

3. Ensure they have provided input on the charter

The charter can be revised and approved every year, if necessary. Be flexible and open to suggestions on how to make the program better every year. You should have built a method to amend the charter into the program from the beginning. But if you didn't, now is the time to include that language. The business may have no changes to add but knowing that their input and concerns have been considered may be all that they are really after.

4. Identify and broaden your list of Stakeholders

You certainly identified some stakeholders when governance was first implemented. But who did you miss? This is a prime opportunity to determine if you have gaps that could be filled.

These gaps might be in the business and they may be in IT. Is your Cloud Architecture and Cybersecurity team included in the governance process? (Do they know you exist?) What about the call-center representatives? Have they been trained on the principles of governance and how they apply to their jobs dealing with customers? Are Human Resources or Finance participating?

Do a full review of both your architecture stack and your business organization charts to ensure that you have engaged and taken feedback from every team in your company.

Governance cannot be something that is only done on a central Data Lake. It must be included in the operating models of every system and every business unit. In some cases, it is the business stewards that need to engage the other business teams. But ensure that they know that this is their responsibility and provide them tools with which to engage. Some sample scripting or a basic Power Point presentation explaining the expected outcomes and answering the "Why" question will help those outreaches go more smoothly.

5. Review the Working Charter document with this broader group of stakeholders and include their feedback.

Now that these additional stakeholders have been identified, get their feedback on the governance program. Find out what additional features or outcomes they may want.

6. Identify any competing or conflicting interests and resolve

Ask all stakeholders to review the program charter from the perspective of the regulations that they are accountable for and ensure that you not only have no conflicts but that you are providing value to them in meeting their obligations.

Set a target goal of having an additional x% (no more than 10% per quarter) of their process and policy documents reviewed each quarter or calendar year. This ensures that over time, all operations within the company are aligned to the charter of the governance organization. It also avoids the feeling of being overwhelmed when looking at the amount of work that needs to be done.

Making governance part of the culture is a huge endeavor that will take years. Patiently making progress is better than your program getting killed because you pushed too hard.

The next five steps are things that you very likely did during the initial planning and implementation phase.

I will list them below for reference. If you missed one, go back and do that now.

7. Sketch out the organizational structure of your governance program.

At this stage, review your organizational structure with a critical eye. Is it working? Is it self-centric or inclusive?

8. Define your milestones

This activity should be completed annually. Governance must grow along with the organization. Each year you should have specific milestones of what you want to improve and how much additional coverage you plan to implement. Like any program, governance should have a 1-, 3- and 5-year roadmap of planned outcomes.

9. Break milestones down into specific deliverables.

Basic Project Management stuff here. Ensure that you have a plan for each milestone. A Milestone two years away may need action this year to make it possible. Break each milestone into steps and components. You may find that operations has already planned a strategic project that is similar in scope or close enough that your governance initiative could piggy-back for maximum benefit and value. Change presented in this manner to the business provides additional benefits they can use in their project business cases.

Conversely, a review of strategic projects could show a significant divergence from the direction needed for better governance. Having a voice in the strategic planning process requires that you know, concretely, what needs to be accomplished, who needs to be involved, and when it needs to be completed. Your planning process should be every bit as detailed as the businesses' strategic plan – perhaps even more detailed.

Ask business leadership for their strategic planning template and guidelines and present information in their language and on their schedule. Of course, run it up your chain's flagpole before presentation to ensure that your leadership and business sponsors agree with your direction before it becomes set in stone. Interference with the strategic planning process can create tensions. But if you have very concrete deliverables and benefits – especially quantifiable benefits, you can be viewed as a valuable ally.

10. Revisit your "Parking Lot" in the planning process
It is normal that as you were implementing your program some items and wish lists didn't make it to the top of the stack. Don't forget about these items. They are a golden opportunity to prove to the business that you listened to their priorities and needs. The Parking Lot from initial implementation is the first place you should look when creating your Roadmap and specific deliverables.

You should also keep a running Parking Lot list. View the suggestions and ideas provided to you as gifts, not distractions. You may decide along the way that an idea is counter to the overall direction or is met in another way. Close the loop with the business stakeholder who provided the idea to build trust. It may not always be evident across the corporate landscape that a project or initiative has fulfilled someone else's need. Being the group that closes the loop and helps maximize project benefits with little effort on their part will set you up as a thought leader.

Eventually you will be included in brainstorming and planning activities that you may not even be aware are happening. Many business groups undertake "Rapid Process Improvement" initiatives under operational funding. Your input could save them valuable time and resources if you can point to other solutions that may exist outside of their view. Taking action items from these initiatives back to the overall Data Steward council may also help strike gold and minimize the effort to make improvements.

11. Turn over to Operations

The initial implementation of the Governance Program should have had a step to turn ownership of information over to Operations. If it didn't, now is the time to do so. If it did, you have an opportunity to strengthen the participation and value provided by the business Data Stewards.

The next section of this chapter goes deeper into Operationalizing the program.

12. Review the working charter with sponsors and stakeholders

This was a pre-implementation step to ensure alignment of purpose and agreement prior to implementing the program. If this step was skipped, as it sometimes is, now would be a good time to get that alignment of purpose.

13. Implementation of the Program

This is a series of steps that should have been followed. The previous sections covered the development necessary to lead to these steps. Use this as a checklist to ensure you have a well-rounded program:

a. Implement the structure of the Governance Organizational
b. Achieve each implementation deliverable according to schedule
c. Mark off each milestone through the Phase Gate review
    i. It's very important to keep track of your wins

    ii. Feedback on these wins helps your stakeholders see the benefits of collaboration

d. Keep the Parking Lot current and begin to put in future dates for planning purposes, as discussed above
e. Develop the long-term Roadmap to implement items outside of the initial scope
f. Develop the artifacts and staffing model needed to turn over to operations

The final three steps are for wrap-up of the implementation and the beginning of continuity.

14. Communicate Successes, Risks, Issues, and Status

The project most likely had a communication plan that shared this kind of information to sponsors along the way. Pull it out and expand upon it to create an ongoing communication program that keeps sponsors, stakeholders, and team members updated continually.

15. Turn over to Operations

This step is almost always sloppy. It is the reason I wrote this book in the first place.

I have been affected by many projects that had brilliant implementation plans, but they did not consider what the program would look like and how it would function after the project team went away.

Completing a project and tossing it over the wall to the business without preparation is the surest way to find that you have wasted a lot of money as your governance program lies rotting on the ground.

Plan for the functional differences between IT and business operations and ensure that the governance program you have built or are building is structured in a compatible manner. The next section in this chapter works through setting Key Performance Indicators for the program. These need to be compatible with the organization structures of both Business and IT.

16. Document your successes and have Business Sponsors approve

While this step sounds like a once-and-done activity, that is only true if you are thinking of setting up the program from the limited perspective of completing a project. If you plan for the long-term sustainability of the governance organization and operations, regular check-ins and approval by the Executive Sponsor, Business Sponsors, Stewards, Stakeholders and team members need to be understood. Whether it is a quarterly report, a semi-annual review or a year-end reset and review, it is critical for your funding and the business funding to show value and progress.

Identify Content Improvements

Business content is governed by policies and procedures and is monitored by audits. This isn't exactly what we think of when we start talking about data dictionaries, classification systems, data lineage, etc. Data is governed by rules, codified structures, and information architecture, all of which fit neatly in the above topics.

So, how can this be reconciled?

There has never been a better time to be asking and answering this question.

The potential of Machine Learning and Artificial Intelligence (AI) can be leveraged to assist in the management and tagging of unstructured data. Systems exist that can access and tag documents, text files, audio files, images and video with metadata, classification, categories, concepts, keywords, entities, and even emotions and sentiment. This idea can be daunting if you are thinking about how much information will suddenly be made available to business users and the potentially overwhelming demand for support from Information Technologists.

But if looked at as an opportunity to provide increased clarity, remove redundancies, streamline utilization and put logical controls around the content utilized by business, suddenly you have a scenario that opens up cost savings and improved analytics.

Let me give you an honest example of why this new capability is so valuable. (This happened to me and it is one reason that I find this so fascinating.)

I do a lot of international business. Buying and selling products and services internationally can be risky. Sometimes things are literally lost in translation when negotiating and sometimes things are lost in the mail. There are also people who intentionally defraud or utilize a transaction to gain access to your personal or financial information.

Earlier this year I purchased an item from an overseas supplier that turned out to be a fake. I returned the item according to the terms of the sale and requested a refund. Without boring you with the long and tedious back and forth details, I had to resort to utilizing the protections on my credit card to resolve the issue. When I called customer service and requested assistance, the nice person on the other end of the phone said, "I can see by the stress in your voice that you are genuine in your concern and giving an honest account of the situation." Wow! This guy had a voice and speech analyzer that inferred that I was both upset and telling the truth! That is Intelligent Automation at work!

Imagine what this kind of system could do for your customer experience scores. I know I was more than impressed, I was wowed! Score a 10 on the Forrester scale for this company!

Utilizing new technologies and concepts are a great way to optimize the control and governance of information.

Another opportunity to optimize the governance program is through conducting a full audit of security protocols. Often redundant processes followed by operations are put in place over time to meet new or changing security policies. Ensuring that you have a joint Business/IT effort to review, merge, and retire processes for security policies will guarantee that you are not violating current regulations and will minimize holes in your security landscape.

A Perfect Governance Structure

In a perfect world all policies would start with a *regulation* or *standard*. Each regulation and standard would be analyzed for compliance terms and a policy written to comply.

Each written *policy* would reference the regulation or standard that is met by this policy.

Each *procedure* would be documented and would reference both the policy and the applicable regulations and/or standards.

A business policy *map* would model the *relationships* of the policies and procedures to the appropriate regulations and standards.

A *summary document* would be attached to the regulation or standard in the repository which provides a map to each policy and procedure utilized to meet the regulation or standard.

Essentially you would have a two kinds of reference maps. One that ties regulations and standards to policies and from there to procedures. And an opposing branching tree diagram would tie each procedure to a policy and regulation or standard.

Each document would also have a *regular review cycle*, the date of origination, date of approval and subsequent review cycle approvals, and the name (or title) of the specific Business Owner of the policy and the procedure.

Of course, this is describing an ideal state as if you could start over with a blank slate and build the processes and policies of an organization from the ground up.

But it is possible to get there over time. Part of the Optimization process could be to choose a single regulation and trace the policies and procedures that fulfill the requirements. I believe you will find it incredibly eye-opening to undertake this exercise.

When you think about optimization of your governance program, first recognize the difference between the way Business and IT think about information. Then identify new technologies that may streamline the governance process for the Business.

And finally, assist the Business in creating an inventory management program and process for policy and procedure documentation.

Once you have taken these steps to Optimize the governance program and provide value to the Business, it is time to lead the effort to Operationalize the governance program.

In the next section we'll cover how to measure your successes through Key Performance Indicators.

Set Key Performance Indicators on the Governance Program

The business is generally held to strict KPI's. Adding KPI's for the governance program to their metrics will be a familiar pattern and will benefit the organization by ensuring that governance is aligned with the standards and methods of general business.

While the specific KPI's you set on your governance program will reflect your maturity model and culture, following are some suggested KPI's that may be adopted by the stewards and business participants in the governance program.

Suggested KPI's:

1. Participate in 80% of governance meetings and action plans
2. Suggest metrics to measure business and IT stewards against that align with the governance program metrics.
3. Set a target goal of having x% (no more than 10% per quarter) of business process and policy documents reviewed each quarter or calendar year.
4. Annual milestones of improvements and/or growth of scope to be implemented in the governance program and operations culture.
5. Set a target for additional penetration of the governance program into operations.

These suggestive KPI's are intended to spark your thinking about how to measure participation in the governance activities.

Measuring the participation and acceptance of the governance program is a major step toward infusing governance into the culture of the organization.

Operationalize Governance

Business hates it when IT steps in and tells them how to run their business. After all, the Key Performance Indicators and reported Metrics for business are usually built around quantity of transactions, which is very measurable, and satisfaction of the customer, which is somewhat subjective.

Business has a perception, mostly accurate, that IT doesn't understand the regulatory or performance factors that drive business decisions or their hunger and need for access and availability of information to utilize for conducting the everyday business of the company.

IT has a perception, mostly accurate, that Business doesn't care about the need to limit user access and data transfer of information for maximum information security and optimization of system performance.

It's almost as if the Business speaks French and IT speaks Spanish. They are both Latin-based languages but are not close enough to bridge the gap of understanding.

You may be asking why you need a bridge. Isn't data governance the provenance of IT? Why should "Business Operations" be involved?

In my first book on this topic, *get Governed*, I defined Data Governance as, "The activity of defining and organizing structure around information." In my many years of experience serving as a bridge between IT and the Business, I had always interacted in a manner that treated Information Governance and Data Governance as synonyms. But this is changing, not just for me, but in the industry.

For a governance program to succeed long-term, it needs to be part of culture of an organization. This is only possible when both Business and IT are working together.

You may be asking what I mean by "operationalize." Many definitions exist, but most of them boil down to, "put into operations." I'm not a huge fan of defining a term with the root word. But in this case, it is accurate.

Definition of "Operationalize"

To "operationalize" governance means to *firmly embed the activities and concepts of governance into the everyday operations of your organization until they become the natural state of performing work and thinking about information.*

If you think about that idea for a moment you may begin to recognize practices in your organization that are not governed. In the next chapter we will discuss Valuing your governance program. But before you can realize the full value of governance, it needs to be deeply engrained in the culture.

Steps to Operationalize

1. Mature the mindset about governance to encourage adoption as a fundamental core

principal of all operations within business and IT
2. Provide Education on the "how" and "why" of using governance
3. Consider offering incentives

Implementing these three concepts will help solidify governance into the culture.

1. Mindset and adoption

Changing the hearts and minds of business requires that you provide a compelling reason to change. The esoteric nature of a governance program can leave the business in a state of denial about the need to participate. But if you can show them the critical nature of their participation, they can become strong proponents and supporters.

As mentioned above, the business generally looks at governance as an IT function. But this is changing.

A new way of thinking and talking about Governance as a practice and a profession has begun to emerge. The Information Coalition, a group of information professionals, not a traditional association, developed an Information Body of Knowledge (InfoBOK) that resonates with me and helped clarify why the task of fully governing information seemed so out of reach for most organizations.

The InfoBOK v.1.0 provided a broad cross-industry definition of Information Governance that resonates with our changing profession and scope. Below is my interpretation of their definition:

> *"Everything is Information. Data is a sub-set of Information that resides in structured systems with pre-defined relationships and definitions. Content is everything else."*

Hence, Data Governance under IT covers the information that resides in structured systems and only accounts for a sub-set of the entire landscape of Information Governance.

Business utilizes masses of Content which is information that is not structured. That information should also be governed. The activity of governing needs to be expanded beyond Data Governance to become Information Governance.

Look at the graphic below. This illustrates the reality of information in any organization and helps elucidate the perspective of the Business.

Figure 2: Content vs. Data

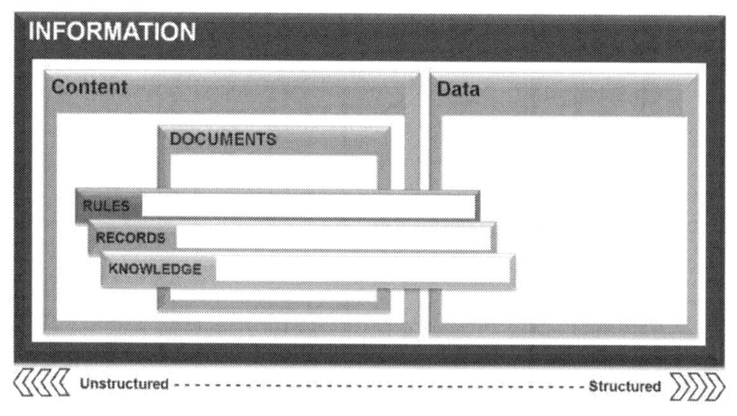

*Information Body of Knowledge, InfoBOK vs. 1.0, page 25, ©Information Coalition 2018

If you are like me, seeing this picture provides a tremendous amount of clarity.

It is no longer a mystery why IT driven and controlled governance initiatives fall on deaf ears within the Business. And it is why your governance program may be stuck without delivering on the benefits that were expected or the ability to grow.

I had a few "A-Hah" moments when I first looked at this picture:

- Most information is Business Content that is unstructured.
- IT has control of a limited amount of information classified as Data.
- Governance programs that don't heavily involve the Business along with their masses of unstructured Content are going to fail and eventually be crushed.
- Privacy and Information Security initiatives that only cover structured information are inadequate at best and failing at worst.
- The Business has a greater accountability for the governance of information than is generally acknowledged. Their accountability is of a broader scope than that of IT.

The need to bring the Business into the governance process and make them EQUAL PARTNERS in governing the information of the company can't come fast enough.

A mistake that I often see is an over-reaction to the new Privacy laws. The CIO sees how much Information the Business controls and has a knee-jerk reaction. Access and Availability are severely limited, and business practically comes to a stand-still. Business lobbies for return of their access while IT frantically struggles to come up with rules and processes for how information should be used. Remember that this is usually done without the input of the Business – the people with the *context* of the information.

When these situations arise, a tension between IT and the Business will become a conflict. Relations break down, business growth slows, and the divide seems almost too great to bridge.

If I may give a word of advice, "PLEASE, DON'T DO THIS!" But if it's already done, revert to the old normal and start again.

Before a revocation of rights is undertaken, ASK. What information does the business need and why? Make Joint decisions about how to limit access. Most business leaders will understand that not everyone on their team needs access. But there are selective analytics groups who do need access that begins to bridge the gap into IT's territory. That is actually a good thing. It means that you have a group who can begin to serve as the ambassadors of governance to the rest of the business community.

Don't remove the access of the very people who need to advocate for your process of governance. Acknowledge their role and educate them on how to govern the unstructured information within their control and how to best identify what structured information is appropriate to have within the governance process.

2. Education and Development

The scenario above illustrates the level of disconnect between the working knowledge and understanding of technical teams and business teams. The technical teams are used to using and familiar with the basic terminologies and concepts of governance, even before formal governance is established. But business users, even those who utilize data and technical queries, such as SQL, to harvest information from various systems are not likely to be familiar with data models, classification terminology, lineage, or other technical ideas. It is critical that you provide a formal education program. You can't assume that because they nod their heads and agree with you that they understood most of what you need from them.

Remember that most of these business analysis team members are not going to be familiar with the architectural terminology that IT uses. Spend intentional time documenting and teaching. This is likely to result in the need for a formally documented and agreed upon set of terminology and methodology across the organization. Start with your own house first. Ensure that all of your team members and your IT colleagues understand and agree with the language you intend to roll out to the business. You may find that even within different silos of the IT organization, definitions and perspectives may differ.

Once the IT side of the house agrees on terminology and methodology, ensure that it is well documented, and a training method has been agreed upon by your governance sponsors and champions within IT and the business. Spend the time to roll the educational program out to the various groups.

Remember that change is most effective when only one thing is changed at a time. Not only does this make it more palatable, but it ensures that you can identify a misstep quickly. When more than one thing is changed, it may be difficult to identify the specific cause of conflicts or misunderstandings.

Education and good change management will go a long way toward better long-term adoption of the program. Recall the phrase, "Go slow so you can go fast." Getting the foundation in place first will allow an acceleration of adoption and a better experience for everyone.

3. Utilize Incentives

If you can avoid the conflict about governance, and you have provided education, you may wish to utilize incentives to bring the business along. Some incentives might be to throw the CIO's support behind business initiatives to modernize their systems, scan their paper documents to digital, or convert unstructured Access databases into structured content. Remember that if you are offering these types of incentives, you need to give the Business assurances that they won't lose their traditional control of the management and context of this information – in other words, they won't lose access to the information that they turn over to IT.

Other incentives may be more tangible. Can you offer promotions or bonuses for new ideas or strong supporters? HR policies and legal considerations need to be followed closely if you go down this route. But money is a great motivator. Other people are driven by status and titles. Investigate if that is an opportunity to garner support. Titles don't always need to be tied to salary. Sometimes a title is simply a way to formally and publicly recognize someone's efforts. This type of incentive can either change the culture or conform to it. But either way, they are effective methods for getting business engaged and committed to the success of the governance program.

Partnership and collaboration are the best ways to ensure that the Business feels empowered to join you in the governance process.

Chapter 4 Summary

In this chapter we discussed how to Optimize and Operationalize your governance program.

To Optimize we focused in two areas:

1. Identifying opportunities to improve your program's functionality
2. Setting Key Performance Indicators (KPIs) to measure the adoption and penetration of governance

We reexamined the implementation *Success Checklist* and identified areas that could be improved. We then looked at how business and IT could adopt joint performance measures on the successful adoption of governance.

Next, we focused on three steps to better Operationalize governance:

1. Maturing the mindset about governance across the entire organization – both IT and business, to encourage adoption as a fundamental core principal of all operations
2. Providing Education on the "how" and "why" of using governance
3. Using an Incentive model to encourage participation and commitment.

By optimizing the program and then ensuring that it is fully operationalized within the business and IT, you have strengthened the position of governance and advanced it as an important part of the company's culture.

Chapter 5 – V = Value the Governance Program

"Good government is one of the most important factors in economic growth and social well-being." – Joe Lonsdale

A governance program provides measurable value to an organization. But in order to actualize that value, Information must be treated as a tangible asset. Have you invested the same level of attention and planning around your information as you have your supply chain or financial assets? Most organizations haven't considered that the information they hold is a supply of kinetic energy just waiting to be released to offer value.

I do want to clarify that the value of Information is not just about the ability to sell it as a product. The primary values are internal. Just as your supply chain transportation methods add value and can be measured as an indicator of company performance, so too can your information flow and usage.

Information that is undiscovered, not controlled, and siloed is stagnant. It is dead weight that holds you back. Opening these vaults and bringing your information into a cohesive framework will allow for the monetization of information.

Before you can monetize your information, you must first ensure that it is identified, managed and available in a manner that aligns with best practices and is compatible with the culture of the organization.

It has been my experience that if you ask the super-SME business analyst how valuable the information is that their department uses, they will tell you it is immeasurable. And in fact, it probably is not measurable due to a missing framework to measure that value. But they couldn't do their job without access to the right information. To change the culture of the organization to one of Governance, winning over the key users of information is critical. Showing them that they matter, and that the strategy is designed to assist them, rather than alienate them, will go a long way to winning supporters and cheerleaders for your efforts.

At this point we should assume that you have taken the time to identify the structured and unstructured information in your company and that you have a plan to manage it according to the overall governance principals you've adopted. Now you need to be able to show the value of your efforts toward a more governed state.

Douglas B. Laney of Gartner, Inc. wrote what I believe to be the definitive book on valuing data: "*Infonomics*" (©Gartner Inc. 2018, published by Bibliomotion, Inc.) explores three key areas to transform information into economics. I highly recommend the book, especially for the advanced governance program. The three sections of "*Infonomics*" cover, in this order:

- Monetizing Information as an Asset
- Managing Information as an Asset, and
- Measuring Information as an Asset

This chapter is not intended to be a summary of Doug's work. In fact, while I respect his work tremendously and it has certainly influenced my thinking, my view of governing information comes from inside the inner workings of many companies' operations teams and not from an external consultant's perspective. My experience has demonstrated that most organizations, if we're being brutally honest here, need to start at a more basic level. This chapter is about valuing the *Program* not the *Information.*

The work you have done to Establish, Build, Grow, Optimize and Operationalize your Governance Program puts you in a position to show the value of your efforts. I recommend measuring and reporting on these four areas:

- Discovery
- Control
- Quality
- Transformation Strategy

Discovery

Before value can be assigned to information, it must first be discovered. The work you have done to identify and classify data, systems, processes, and data flows should give you a sense of the scope of the information stored in company assets – systems, file cabinets, and tribal knowledge. Once you have that view you can begin to measure how much of the information is governed.

A simple method for measuring the depth of the governance effort could look something like this:

> *Report of the Discovery of Information Assets of XYZ company as of September 15, 2016:*
>
> - *Structured Data sources: 211*
>   - *Unique Transaction systems: 21*
>   - *Data transportation systems and middleware: 185*
>   - *Data warehouse systems: 5*
> - *Unstructured Information sources: 3,567*
>   - *Electronic Document storage: 45 repositories*

- *Business-controlled Access databases: 2,537*
- *Business-controlled SQL databases: 963*
- *File cabinet storage (paper):*
  - *22 banks*
  - *932 drawers*
  - *7,000 files (estimated or counted)*
- *Tribal knowledge centers: 15 consisting of a total of 80 Super-SME subject matter experts*

This basic level of discovering the information in your organization provides a baseline against which to measure your governance penetration. The discovery process can and should go deeper, of course. Each of the identified sources should be evaluated for overlap and redundancy. There is also a necessary tension between access and security that must be considered. This should be measured against the core foundational principals of your governance strategy and security policies. Let's go through a very simplified exercise to illustrate how to do this analysis and how to measure value from the discovery process.

Discovery example 1 – Customer data

In your discovery process you find that four main transactional systems hold customer data:

1. Customer database containing:
    a. Business or Individual Name
    b. Billing Address
    c. Shipping Address
    d. Order History
    e. Contact information, i.e. email, phone, website, etc.
2. Shipping database containing:
    a. Name
    b. Shipping Address
    c. Special delivery information, i.e. Saturday delivery okay, Attn: Marlene, Post Office Box only
3. Payment/Billing database containing:
    a. Customer name
    b. Billing name

c. Billing address
d. Contact information
e. Payment method, i.e. credit card information, invoice instructions or bank debit information
f. Contract terms such as 30-day invoice, outstanding balances, credits, etc.

4. Contract database containing:
    a. Contracting entity name
    b. Business name
    c. DBA names or Aliases
    d. Contact information for contract signer
    e. Contract terms including rates, invoice agreement, payment agreements, arbitration or legal agreements, etc.

When placed into a spreadsheet, it is easy to see that a large amount of the information captured and used seems to be duplicated between these systems.

Figure 3: Database Comparison Chart Example

Glossary Term	Databases:			
	Customer Database	Shipping Database	Payment/Billing Database	Contract Database
Contracting Entity Name				Y
Business Name	Y		Y	Y
Individual Name	Y		Y	
DBA Name				Y
Shipping Name		Y		
Billing Address	Y		Y	
Shipping Address	Y	Y		
Order History	Y			
Contact information	Y		Y	
Contracting Contact				Y
Special Delivery Information		Y		
Payment Method			Y	
Contract Terms			Y	Y

Create a checklist for comparison that includes items such as:

- Consult or document the Information Glossary to ensure that terms are used in consistent manners.
- If terminology matches, investigate the business processes or policies around the terms.
- Create a business standard for the collection and maintenance of the information. i.e. alpha-numeric rules,

mixed case or upper case, date format, etc.

- Identify if any of the information is fed to a data lake or data warehouse. If so, can it be accessed in a publication/ subscribe type of data sharing?
- Where does the information integrate with other systems? Is it passed along, or does it require duplicate data entry?

Once you have the answers to these questions you can begin to document the waste or saving of manhours involved with the duplicate information.

Calculate these factors:

1. Number of hours to manage the information. Multiply by the number of times the information is managed. Add any additional time spent modifying or changing the information as it is used across departments. Times by the

standard hourly rate. = Cost of the duplicate information.

<u>This number is a "Value" of the Discovery process of Governance.</u>

2. Where information is not flowing from team to team, what is the cost to build an automated ETL integration between systems or a "call" to a publication database? Is that cost per year more or less than the manual cost to maintain the information? (Remember that this needs to be multiplied by the standard strategic NPV length – usually 3 or 5 years)

   <u>This number is another "Value" of the Discovery process of Governance.</u>

3. If different policies exist between departments and this is regulated information by some governing or accredited organization, what is the legal risk of having information stored that is not in compliance? Have you paid any fines in the past? Are there

industry benchmarks on the cost of potential fines if this is discovered?
This cost avoidance is a "Value" of the Discovery process of Governance.

As you can see, it is not difficult to come up with scenarios for how to value the Discovery of the information in your organization.

Control

The process of Discovery leads smoothly into the process of Control. As you evaluated policies and regulations you should have identified a list of information that needs to be governed. The value of Control of these sources is measured in much the same way as Discovery. The main factors you will consider are:

1. Is there a regulation and what is the potential financial risk?
2. What is the process to put controls and governance around the information?

3. How much time will governance require on a monthly or annual basis, valued in cost per manhour?
4. Is there a Benefit after completing the cost/benefit analysis?

Controlling information may be as simple as documenting that it is reviewed and that a review cycle is in place. It may be as complicated as developing AI or Machine Learning algorithms to monitor and alert when information is no longer within the set parameters.

Control, of all the values of governance, is the most open to subjective determination. You will find that your legal department, risk management and cybersecurity teams will be great allies in determining what needs to be controlled and what "Control" means for your organization.

Quality

Quality of information is often lumped into "Data Quality." Most organizations have department specific data quality programs. These include activities such as file audits, processor audits, policy audits, or automated consistency audits, such as date formats or extra spaces pulled by manual report and evaluated.

Few organizations have full-scale data quality programs that evaluate the information across the enterprise to ensure consistency and accuracy. The Value of governance of Quality is primarily around this enterprise view.

In my previous book, *get Governed: Building World Class Data Governance Programs* (©Morgan Templar 2017, published by Ivory Lady Publishing), I provided nine dimensions of Information Quality.

Nine Dimensions of Information Quality

1. **Conformed**: Does it conform to the data standards (i.e. MM/DD/YYY for date or ###-##-#### for Social Security Number)
2. **Valid**: Beyond Conformance, does the information make sense. For example: year in a date is within the expected range (2103 vs 2013) or no dummy values such as 999-99-9999 for SSN.

3. **Complete**: No missing values
4. **Accurate**: Requires an authoritative source to compare against. Sometimes called "correct."
5. **Consistent**: is the information the same between systems/applications
6. **Unique**: If expected, is the information unique within the data set
7. **Available**: Is the information accessible and/or was the application running during business hours or according to Service Level Agreements
8. **Timely**: Was the information entered into the system or application in a manner that complied with turnaround times or SLAs
9. **Current**: How likely is the information to represent "Now"

Taking these nine concepts to the Enterprise level will illuminate the very likely circumstance that each department, team or function measures these things differently. The value of the governance program is in creating standard measures, standard values, and consistent reporting of the quality of information.

In the process of implementing this overarching view of quality you will encounter some resistance. Most business teams have some KPI or individual performance standard around the quality of the information they manage. If the rules around that information change, you should expect to see a dip in the current quality metric being reported by some teams. Make sure that this expectation of a dip is clearly communicated both to senior leadership, and the individuals who are being measured. There is no sense in creating an unnecessary panic when a team that has consistently self-reported their quality score as 99% or greater for the past ten years suddenly has a score of 67%.

You may be asking, "How would that happen?" A scenario just like this occurred with one of my operational teams. For more than ten years they had measured their quality in audits versus information received. They did not have any way to compare the information against another trusted source to verify truth (measured as "consistency" in the Nine Data Quality Dimensions). Measuring quality in this way was built into performance scores of each individual processor and affected their pay and bonuses.

In 2015, a regulatory agency changed its quality audit methodology to consider the entire record inaccurate if even one of the five key data components were inaccurate. When the records were sent to a third-party auditor who compared the information to their internal data set, the results were a score of 67% accurate.

A drop of 33% is huge and was shocking to executives and processors alike. The operations manager over the team nearly had a heart attack because he had worked very hard to develop his team to what had been considered a benchmark nationally. This new way of measuring was not only a surprise to him, but to everyone involved.

It's important for a governance process to consider that implementing a new standard of quality or a new measurement methodology is going to result in different scores. The important thing is to communicate clearly to all involved and provide a window or roadmap for adjusting to the new methods. Processes and policies may need to be changed. KPI's, Metrics, and Personal Performance Goals may need to be reset. Stakeholders need to be informed and communication plans created and followed.

The value of governance in this process can be measured by satisfaction surveys, including surveys taken on a quarterly basis, feedback from employee performance evaluations, the "Great Place to Work" type of annual surveys in questions such as "Expectations of my job are clearly defined," and with other methods of feedback.

Once a standard method of measuring quality has been identified and implemented across all teams, the financial aspects of the improvement can be measured against potential fine avoidance or other cost-avoidance measures.

Transformation Strategy

Highly successful companies are highly strategic and competitively modernized. The ability to transform an organization effectively relies on the ability to identify, communicate and implement change in an effective and intentional manner.

The governance organization offers the potential to measure the value of transformation. Intentional change requires active participation by all sides of the organization. IT can't force something on the business; one team can't toss their problems over the wall downstream to the next team; quality can't be ignored; cost must be considered and weighed.

The value of the governance organization is in being a central group where standards can be established and progress measured. It provides increased transparency and the opportunity for participation. It normalizes change into part of the culture instead of allowing it to damage the culture.

Think about your transformation strategy. Who sets the direction? Who analyzes the impacts? Who evaluates the cost of those impacts? And how is that measured across differing initiatives? Is each Project Manager or Business Driver allowed (or required) to determine costs and benefits of a business case alone in a bubble? Or is there a standard method that should be utilized?

I suggest that the Governance Organization is the ideal place to hold those standards and ensure that they are followed through the strategic planning process. This is not to say that an analytic control organization should be supplanted. It does mean that the processes and decisions will be monitored and reported on for consistency and value to the governance organization. In this way, the true weighted value of changes and transformations can be established, measured, and improved over time.

Chapter 5 Summary

In this chapter we discussed how to show the value of the Governance Organization through measuring and reporting on four areas:

- Discovery
- Control
- Quality
- Transformation Strategy

This is not about measuring the value of your stored Information. The value offered by governance supports business cases, strategic portfolios, legal compliance, efficient operations, and consistent, transparent reporting of metrics, KPI's and individual performance measures.

These benefits and values are both financial and subjective in ways such as satisfaction and reputation.

Chapter 6 – E = Evolve the Governance Program

"Every once in a while, a new technology, an old problem, and a big idea turn into an innovation." – Dean Kamen

Most of the topics we have covered have been centered around a fairly loose governance structure that takes a federated approach to governance. The evolution of Privacy and Security regulations, the expansion of the use of Artificial Intelligence and Machine Learning and innovative niche solutions for data and information challenges are driving governance programs to evolve.

Every organization will have different areas where they are strong or weak. As the technology that we use for business changes rapidly, it is critical that a core foundation has been laid for governance. Once that foundation is in place, evolving and expanding into a broader oversight role within the organization will offer additional benefits.

At its core, governance boils down to four key ideas:

- Order
- Structure
- Discipline
- Control

These key ideas should be a part of every conversation about information or business process. The governance team should become an integral part of every change. I push for Governance to be a "C" (or Consulted) on every program/project RACI (Responsible, Accountable, Consulted, Informed matrix).

Every new policy, regulation, rule, strategic decision, or process should consider your guiding governance framework. The resource needs for this level of infiltration isn't sustainable if the governance organization must be represented during the design of each of these changes. That is why having governance as part of the culture is so critical. The governance organization, by way of the data stewards and/or data owners should *ALWAYS* be part of formal programs and projects. Otherwise you end up with duplicate artifacts (such as glossaries), inconsistent data dictionaries or poor process or audit decisions that demand remediation to bring the operation back into alignment within governed parameters. As you speak about your program these four terms should roll off your tongue naturally and regularly. Get people to talk the talk to reinforce walking the walk.

Order

Is to put governance into practice. It is a combination of the noun and the verb "order." The Noun is "the arrangement or disposition of people or things in relation to each other according to a particular sequence, pattern, or method." And the Verb is "to give an authoritative direction or instruction to do something." Said another way, *Order* is a Directive to perform a task, in this case governance, in a specific sequence, pattern or method.

When order is instilled in the *normal* process, then it is cultural. Evaluating those processes of how things get done and ensuring that they align with the principles put in place by the governing organization is critical.

For example, the normal process of defining a Standard Operating Procedure (SOP) includes the recognition of a need – either through solution design or gap analysis, the collection of requirements – both business and technical/system, the creation of a business process diagram, definition of the terms used, and development of written and/or pictorial instructions on the content to put in a system field. The Order implied by governance is the recognition and practice of following approved methodologies. The solution or gap analysis process would involve business experts and technical resources aligning on a process that conforms to information and data architectural standards as well as meeting the regulatory, business or strategic needs of the business. Similarly, a process defined because of an identified gap would have specific ties to closing the reason the gap analysis was performed in the first place, often due to missed or new regulatory requirements. The process to define the procedure should include referencing the business data model to ensure that the flow of the procedure aligns with the up- and down-stream processes, both business and technical, and a requirement to upload the business process diagram to the business process engineering repository. It also includes referencing the approved business glossary for terminology definitions to ensure consistent understanding. And the instructions for the entry of information should support the processes and reasons for each of these identified areas.

The same controls should occur when defining a rule, capability, solution, or readiness plan.

Structure

The outcome of providing structure should be a defined consistent pattern or organization in the arrangement of and relations between the parts or elements of something complex.

A simple method of achieving structure is the development of a checklist or other guiding documentation that gives understandable and consistent direction. A more complicated model is the Integrated Solution View (ISV). The ISV provides the workflow of the process, the applicable, rules, and the appropriate data definitions. These are generally housed in a central repository and should be related to the reference architecture of the organization.

Discipline

The purpose of discipline is consistency. If we consider discipline to be a branch of knowledge studied, usually when referring to higher education, we begin to see that it is less about a punitive method to train someone to conform to a behavior and is more about creating an understanding and the following agreement through training and practice.

Discipline requires work and constant vigilance. It is easy to get lazy and not follow the proper process. But the good news is that once the discipline becomes the method that the people in the organization reference in their speech and activities, the monitoring of activities becomes much easier and information and data practices are naturally easier.

Control

Think of control as a method and authority to influence behavior or the course of events while taking into account extraneous factors that might affect the results.

Control is often achieved by audits. But audits are retrospective methods of control and by their nature generally only sample and measure.

A better method of control aligns well with Agile processes. The "acceptance criteria" of a requirement or "user story" should dictate that the appropriate governing activity was performed. When governance is part of the requirements for completion, your teams will be far more anxious to engage you rather than you having to chase them.

These four concepts – Order, Structure, Discipline, and Control, will provide a framework for you to evolve your program and more firmly entrench governance into "the way things get done."

Expansion

Beyond the methods described above to evolve the program, there are four rapidly changing functions that can benefit greatly from inclusion in the governance process:

- Issue Resolution
- Audit Response
- Cybersecurity
- AI and Machine Learning

Issue Resolution

Every organization has data issues. Loss of content or context as information travels through its lifecycle are common and expected. Have you ever played the game "telegraph?" The content and context lost by passing a simple word or phrase through multiple people is always surprising and often comical. But there is nothing comical about it when you are talking about information or contextual accuracy.

A typical method of issue resolution is to put in an IT Help Desk ticket. But how does IT know what priority to assign to each issue? What is critical for the person entering the ticket might seem to the IT resource, considering the big picture, a relatively insignificant incident.

The governance organization is the perfect vehicle to develop and enforce an incident and issue hierarchy that relies on scoring the *impact* of the data issue rather than the *influence* of the person or team reporting the issue.

Before beginning the design or implementation of an Issue Resolution center, do some investigation to find other centers within the organization that may have something similar in place. To be honest, I would be shocked if more than a handful of organizations have enterprise-wide issue resolution. I would be completely unsurprised to hear that each little siloed issue resolution group *thinks* that they are an enterprise solution.

Many large projects implement formal issue resolution processes as part of their scope. Most of those groups dissolve once the project is complete. In the case of a very large implementation, the core group may continue to meet and work on issues indefinitely. There are two problems with this kind of structure. First, this group is no longer governed by a set of rules or oversight of a project team to keep their decisions in line with changes in strategic direction. Second, while this kind of group may think they are addressing all issues, chances are extremely high that they are limited in scope to a single transactional system's issues, or a single team's processes, or the specific issues related to a recurring audit response. This leaves the issues with information or processes that fall outside of the limited scope with no place to go.

Another problem arises from this kind of informal issue resolution team - the duties and time spent working on these issues may not be aligned with the specific job descriptions or productivity metrics of the involved people or teams. This can lead to challenges in performance reviews for participants who are performing at a high level in many areas but are prevented from excelling in their job functions in other areas due to bandwidth issues. Either they will short-change their department or the issue resolution team. This is not ideal for any team member or group.

For the governance team to take on issue resolution, however, it is vital that these pocket groups are included and that their lessons learned are a part of the structure of any future endeavor. It is common that these same people are tapped to be Information/Data Stewards due to their deep subject matter expertise and willingness to solve problems. If they are not officially Information/Data Stewards, it may be beneficial to work with their leadership to have them assigned to your governance team in a direct or dotted line manner.

Ensure that the participants of the issue resolution group have support, permission, and authority to make decisions. And then develop a framework and structure that automates the scoring or weight of each individual issue.

One governance team that I led developed a weighted scoring system utilizing a Fibonacci sequence to provide the weights. We brainstormed a list of important consequences, discussed and agreed on common definitions for each consequence and then ranked them from least impactful to most impactful. We assigned the sequential value from the Fibonacci sequence to each consequence. From there, the consequence questions became a part of submitting a ticket through the Help Desk system. Issues would arrive at our committee already weighted. We only had to review and prioritize those with equal scores for resolution.

The weighting factors we included were broad and likely applicable to most industries, although this was a healthcare organization. Following is a sample of some of our weighted questions:

- Is this a customer facing impact?
- Does this affect access to medical care for 1 or more members?
- Does this issue impact the organization financially more than $1 Million?
- Does this issue impact the organization financially more than $500,000?
- Is there a regulatory impact that this issue affects?

- Is there a public perception impact?
- Does this negatively impact the Mission or Vision of our organization?
- Does this involve a technical issue? i.e. is the system down or not functioning?
- Does this impact more than one team? More than three teams?
- Has this issue been on the list more than 1 month? More than 3 months? More than 6 months? (Aging weights ensure that some issues don't always stay at the bottom of the list)

You get the idea. As a governance body, we reviewed the impact questions, assigned them weighted values and set them up in a ticketing system. Our Issue Stewards met every week for 1 – 2 hours to review, evaluate and assign new tickets and monitor the progress on open tickets. We also reported to our Governance Executive Steering Committee and other Stakeholders on the number and type of issues that were opened and the progress toward completion.

Issues are often a hidden cost in an organization and providing transparency and resolution to them in a logical and acceptable manner is a tremendous benefit to most companies.

Audit Response

Most organizations have an Internal Audit department that review matters such as conflict of interest and separation of duties. They may also be responsible for investigations into negative audit findings from external agencies. In some organizations, it is the legal team or specific operations team that responds to these agency or customer audits.

At one point in the past few years I was accountable to Internal Audit to answer the findings from the Center for Medicare/Medicaid Services (CMS) and concurrently to answer inquiries directly to a customer and a file audit by the National Committee for Quality Assurance (NCQA) on the contents of credentialing files and my team's compliance with their accreditation standards. I had no group within the company to ensure that my answers aligned to our company standards nor that they were consistent. I also needed data from several systems for these different audits. Getting that information was a matter of my ability to *influence* the team, not a matter of the *impact* of the problems that would arise if I couldn't get it in time to meet the time constraints I was held to by each entity.

As you may imagine, it was not only stressful, but it felt a bit roguish to "make it up as I go" with each of these audit responses.

A well-run governance organization could have considered the full scope of my situation and provided the assistance in data acquisition, analysis of each inquiry, and development of consistent responses. Additionally, they could have documented both the inquiries and the responses and provided an opinion about the appropriateness of both the audit and our response based on the contracts or requirements of each entity. They could have taken it a step forward and evaluated how to incorporate the response into current and future design of processes or information repositories.

Cybersecurity

It goes without saying that cybersecurity is crucial in today's environment. From Congressional hearings to social media gossip, how information is handled, managed and secured are hot topics.

The governance organization should be partnering with the information security team to ensure that the requirements of security are understood and met by the various business teams. Conversely, the need to have access to information to perform the essential duties of their jobs is an important business perspective that should be communicated to the security team. Information stewards should meet regularly with representatives from the Information Security team. The mutual support and partnership will make the job of the security team easier and help the business teams accept the constraints necessary for security in a workable manner.

The explosion of ephemeral communication in today's business platforms makes the decisions of Information Security more and more challenging. What is considered a "business conversation?" What is required to be encrypted? Conversations on Slack? What about recorded Zoom or WebEx calls? Do they all need to be catalogued and/or archived? As groups move to the "cloud," do local copies need to be purged? How secure is a "bring your own device" policy? What about access to email and texting on non-company phones?

There are so many questions not included here and so many more that will come up as business becomes more digital.

As a cross-functional enterprise oversight team, the governance organization is in a good position to advise Information Security, Information and Security Architecture, and Encryption services on trends and uses of information and devices that they may not be aware of across the enterprise. The governance stewards are also an excellent sounding board for these IT security teams to plan the rollout of new technology and services.

Artificial Intelligence and Machine Learning

AI and ML are transforming business into one of algorithms and smart language. Decisions of increasing complexity are being made, not by human brains - gray matter, but by computer brains - silicon matter.

There is no previous information or data use case that is stronger for governance than this one.

A person can make a judgement call based on past experiences or on the obvious error, i.e. too many decimal places or 2031 as a date rather than 2013. And while all of those kinds of parameters can be programmed into an AI algorithm and a good ML program can learn to make those decisions by watching and mimicking the behavior of human operators, none of today's technologies can replace a human, just yet. I have seen ML programs that can identify emotion and truthfulness and even make inferences about the emotional state of the person on a call based on language used, volume and tone of voice, and other factors. But those things first had to be observed and somebody had to agree that the outcome of that programming aligned with expectations.

This is where the governance team comes in. Cues are available when working with any customer. Coming to an agreement on what those cues signify and the appropriate response that aligns with the customer satisfaction goals of the organization should be overseen by the cross-functional governance team.

Today we are beginning to explore Blockchain and Smart Contracts. A further evolution of letting our systems be secure and smart.

These are fantastic technologies and a brilliant direction to go for business. But before we get to a computer deciding if our customer is happy, we need to know what a happy customer sounds and acts like AND we need to be able to quantify the value of a happy customer to justify the expense and investment into these new technologies.

The governance organization should be partnering with Enterprise Architecture to review use cases and identify extended or additional value that may exist by implementing these advanced solutions.

Chapter 6 Summary

Information is changing – types, uses, management and in so many other ways. Evolving the governance program on a continual basis to meet the needs of this transformation is crucial. Governing areas such as Issue Resolution, Audit Response, Cybersecurity, and Artificial Intelligence and Machine Learning will add a layer of security and ease of implementation to the advancing technological era. Using the guiding principles of Order, Structure, Discipline and Controls give us a method to ensure our evolving programs become cultural norms.

Chapter 7 – R = Revisit Core Principles

"One of the core organizing principles of my life is that success comes through a delicate balance between making things happen and letting things happen." – Robin S. Sharma

Your governance program is humming along, and you have integrated well with both IT and business teams. It's time to look at your guiding principles and make sure that your governance organization is still meeting the needs for which it was originally established. Pull out your Charter document. Have you evolved beyond those first ideas of what governance should look like? Is it time to update some of the roles and responsibilities? Do you have enough people or perhaps too many?

Asking these and other applicable questions will ensure that governance doesn't become irrelevant. A regular schedule of reviewing the foundations of governance, the processes and team should be written into an annual review cycle. A sure method of killing governance is to let it become stagnant. Another sure killer is to make unnecessary changes. Sometimes culture needs time to grow and to let the good things you hope for happen organically. It is important to keep that perspective and use discernment to avoid both churn and stagnation. It's a delicate balance.

Regular review and revising the operating principles will:

- Keep the team on track
- Ignite excitement for what's coming next
- Mature the program

Keep the team on track

Participation in governance can sometimes feel like an unnecessary redundancy. Reviewing the reasons for governance with the team as well as leadership will remind everyone of the reasons for an active governance organization.

Each team member should be given an opportunity to provide feedback. Think of this like an annual performance review. What does the team think is working and where do they feel the program could improve?

Governance meetings that are monotonous or that rehash the exact same topics week after week will quickly find that attendance starts to drop, objectives are not being met, and leadership begins questioning the expense.

Get feedback from stakeholders and hear their praise and the complaints. Pass these on to the governance team. Let them feel engaged in resolutions and have some ownership in the success.

Keeping the team on track is an important step in building a high-performing team.

Ignite Excitement

The field of governance is growing and expanding faster than you can imagine. It is important that your team can participate in industry events and learn from others who may be going through similar situations. Involvement in organizations such as the

Data Governance Professional Association (DGPO), Association of Intelligent Information Management (AIIM), Association of Records Managers and Administrators (ARMA), American Health Information Management Association (AHIMA), Association of Quality Professionals (AQP) or one of the many other groups that offer conferences, exclusive member benefits, educational opportunities, networking events, certifications and other benefits.

Encouraging participation in one or more of these groups provides a sense of camaraderie and legitimacy to the work of governance. While there is not a single "Golden" set of standards for governance, just yet, there are several Bodies of Knowledge that are utilized (DMBoK, INFOBoK, EIMBok, TOGAF, PMBoK and many others) to help guide the profession and standardize processes.

Request funding to support your information stewards with their membership dues, conference participation, and leadership opportunities within these organizations. You will find that they offer an opportunity for your work to be recognized and/or benchmarked within the governance industry. With permission and support from your legal/communications teams, sign up to share your successes and challenges with your peers at these conferences.

Give your team members who attend these conferences the opportunity to share summaries of presentations they attended with those who had to stay behind.

Being part of something bigger than yourself is very motivating. And positive press from these organizations can go a long way to making you a thought leader in the industry.

Mature the Program

Building external and internal credibility is an important step in the maturing of a governance program. By revisiting your core principles, you can identify what has worked and what has been a challenge.

Keeping up with your industry peers is also an important part of having a mature program. There are several different maturity models available for you to use as a template when you are a member of one of the associations listed above.

A few components should be part of any maturity plan:

- Set clear objectives
- Have a defined roadmap to achieve objectives
- Communicate frequently and with great transparency
- Success and Failures measured against expected outcomes
- Benefit assignment and support for strategic projects should be accessible and pervasive

There are many more, but these, at least, should be part of the maturity model.

Let your senior leadership and sponsors weigh in on both the progress and the future of the program.

Don't let your success be your downfall!

A well-oiled machine is often forgotten. Remember it is the squeaky wheel that gets the grease. Make sure your "squeak" of success is visible and heard regularly. Become indispensable rather than invisible.

A successful governance organization should be concerned with Order, Structure, Discipline, and Controls. Your maturity model should be checking each of these concepts regularly.

Let's take a look at an example of a maturity model developed by Gartner.

Figure 4: Gartner Maturity Model

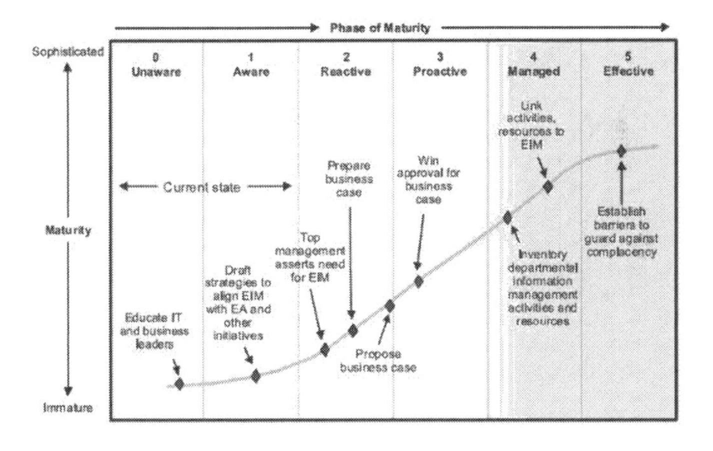

*https://www.gartner.com/doc/846312/overview-gartner-introduces-eim-maturity

Notice that maturity is defined in phases transitioning from Unaware to Effective. Decide what it means to be Unaware, Aware, Reactive, Proactive, Managed, and Effective. Define specific criteria and measure your organization against them on a regular cycle.

Chapter 7 Summary

Keeping your team on track, encouraging their growth and participation in the industry and developing a program maturity model are important aspects of a successful program.

A regular review of your expected outcomes and operating model will allow for continuously updated roadmaps and a voice in the strategic planning cycle.

Chapter 8 – N = Neutralize Naysayers

"If you want to do something different, you're going to come up against a lot of naysayers." – James Dyson

Every organization has someone who is a Negative Nellie. They have nothing but criticism to offer and may complain loudly about, "What a waste it is to invest in this governance thing!" "Just more red-tape!" "I can Google everything they ever 'teach' me."

Have you ever heard any of those complaints? If you have, hopefully they are not coming from one of your senior leaders. But regardless of their level of influence in the company, negative voices often have more weight than they should.

It is very important that you neutralize the negativity. Nothing will kill your program faster. Remember that your goal is to get governance to be part of your culture, or said another way, everyday business should be guided by governance.

Mimicking negative is, unfortunately, a strong human tendency. If left unchecked, a single negative voice can do incredible harm in a short period of time.

As soon as you become aware of a naysayer, you need to address them immediately.

If they are not obvious, they are more dangerous. The hidden negative will eat away at the confidence and support for your program. You must know how to identify those who are not on your side and work to win them over.

Ask yourself a few questions:

- Who are the critics of our program?
- What are they criticizing?
- How can I get them to support us?

Not every criticism is unjustified. Listening to the critics can be an important learning opportunity. Sometimes you improve far more by addressing a criticism than through any planned proactive goal.

But criticism can also be unjustified. Sometimes decisions are made that are not fully transparent to everyone. There are levels of information that really are on a "need to know" basis. And strict governance around that kind of information is common, but often misunderstood.

When you have a critic, it is ideal to engage with them immediately and one on one. Try to avoid group confrontations or ambushes.

Ask them about their criticism. Find ways to work with them to address their concerns. If it simply isn't possible, explain the reasons as much as you can. You may need to involve a senior management representative who can validate that the naysayer has been heard, but also support your direction. Lending that extra bit of authority is an important function of your steering committee and executive sponsor. Give them the opportunity to support you.

If you have attempted to remove the negativity, and have not succeeded, try sending someone else. We all have different communication styles. Sometimes we just don't click with someone. Do you have a team member that perhaps knows or works well with this person? Can they be counted on to stay positive and not be swayed to the negative? If so, ask them to meet with your naysayer.

Inappropriate as it may be, sometimes the negativity is personal. The naysayer may have a problem with you specifically and are simply dumping on the program as a proxy.

Listen to what they are criticizing. Honestly evaluate their comments. Is there merit there? You may find that they have thrown gold nuggets at your program. Don't mistake them for rocks!

If you do find that there is value in the criticism, engage the naysayer in the solution. This will often transform them into allies or champions for the program.

Everyone likes to be validated. They like to know that they have been heard. Give them recognition for the great ideas and show everyone that you are open to innovation and disruption. Both innovation and disruption can seem negative, but they are critical for advancement!

Sometimes the criticism is not valid. That doesn't mean that it will stop just because you have pointed out that it's not valid. You may need to escalate and have a senior leader address the naysayer. Ensure that they are armed with the history of the negativity, your attempts to resolve it, and any concerns about the success of your program before you send them off to advocate on your behalf. The worst possible outcomes sometimes occur by not preparing the leader in advance. You absolutely don't want them to be swayed by the arguments of negativity. The best possible outcome is that your leader will have won over a new ally. You should work hard to grow that new alliance as a way to show gratitude.

Above all, never be the negative one. Whether you are leading the program or are a team member, it is your highest responsibility to be a good ambassador and steward of the governance program. Take every complaint as an opportunity to make something better.

Chapter 8 Summary

Turning your critics into champions is the ultimate victory! But it is just as important to neutralize negativity. Positively engage with those who criticize your program, the work of governance or you specifically. Listen, hear, address, and follow up with them. Be a positive voice for your team and the process. Engage support from your leadership for the unmovable negative and take care to nurture the relationship with newly won allies.

Chapter 9 – Conclusion

"Be not preoccupied with legacy nor popularity. Lead based on core conviction and strong principles and the belief that time and distance will allow for context." – Mark McKinnon (paraphrased)

Governance is one of the keystones of the future of electronic and digital business. Whether your program is new, established or somewhere in between, ensuring that you have a Culture of Governance will set you, and your company, up for a brighter future.

This book has focused heavily on engaging the business team in the process and act of governance. The collaboration and synergy that can be built through the relationship building process will have positive impacts far beyond your governance process.

Many organizations are switching to an Agile framework for both projects and operations initiatives. The introduction of Scrum and Kanban into the culture can be a tremendously valuable change that can be ridden to cement governance as a way of life for both business and IT.

Cultural shifts are challenging. And many people will advocate for one thing at a time. I agree with that sentiment to a point. But governance is different. It applies to each of these segments as they are developed and implemented. It isn't "another thing." It is a critical building block for every "thing" that is done.

A long-term goal of governance would be to go back and identify any processes, policies, rules, or operational functions that don't have an aspect of governance, and then remediate them to be well-governed processes. But it is far more important and possible to start from now and implement governance from where you are today and going forward.

By following these six principles you can GOVERN to greatness:

- G = Grow the Program
- O= Optimize and Operationalize
- V = Value the Program
- E = Evolve the Program
- R = Revisit Core Principles
- N = Neutralize Naysayers

It's an exciting time to be a part of the governance profession. New technologies, the massive need for industries such as healthcare to modernize, and the increased scrutiny on Privacy and Security are fuel in our fire!

Do you remember when email was new? We all wondered what we would do with it. It seemed like such an unnecessary bother. Imagine business today without email! My greatest hope is to look back on this time in business and see that governance has become as much a part of the culture as email.

I wish you good luck, good fortune and GOOD GOVERNANCE!

Acknowledgements

Writing this book has been much more difficult than writing *get Governed.* Many people have influenced my thinking. I would like to thank the clients of Get Governed, LLC in 2018. The focus of this book is centered around the issues you are facing. It is my great honor to have helped to improve your governance programs.

My deep gratitude goes out to the many people who purchased and reviewed *get Governed*, making it an international best seller in several categories. Your tweets, comments through my website, and personal interaction at conferences has fueled my continued passion for better governance!

I am incredibly grateful for Ken Lownie of EverTeam for writing the foreword of this book. He and his team, Barb Mosher Zinck and Margaret Mottolo, have been great collaborators and encouragers. I have enjoyed every minute!

Many others have given me a platform to continue to evangelize governance and I am grateful for each opportunity. Special mention goes out to: Chris LaCour, of Ing3nious; Nick Inglis, of Information Coalition/InfoGov; Abe Gong, of Superconductive Health; Andrew Kobylinski, of BetterDoctor; and Ken Lownie, of EverTeam.

I would be remiss if I didn't thank Marie and Will Crump from Datum and Nanci Ziegler from Change Healthcare for your unwavering support and friendship!

My eternal and forever thanks to my life/soulmate – Stephen Templar. Thank you for tireless encouragement, wicked sense of humor, amazing graphic and editing skills, and being the best friend and love that anyone could ever ask for!

For all of these and many more, I say a huge and tremendous THANK YOU!

And that Thanks extends to all of you reading this book. Your support is very much appreciated. (A review on Amazon would also be appreciated!)

About the Author

Morgan Templar has always been fascinated by the way things work. From electronics to musical instruments, the inner workings of the human mind and the massive public relations/social media movements in society, she is entranced by the similarities, patterns, and rhythms that cross topic and boundaries. She describes herself as a specialist at being a generalist.

Morgan has worked in finance, technology and healthcare. She has held many titles and excelled at many things, but always seems to find a way to focus on rules, structures, and efficiency. Governance, quality, continuous improvement and process efficiency are music to her ears and are the hum of a well-oiled machine.

Morgan is the Chief Executive Officer of Get Governed LLC. She provides consultation services to solve governance, quality and data issues and regularly speaks at conferences on a variety of business topics. She has a Master of Science in Health Administration from The Ohio University and a Bachelor of Science in Public Relations from the University of Utah.

Morgan lives with her husband, Stephen, in Rescue, CA on thirteen acres of holly, chestnut and oak forest with a view of the mountains surrounding Lake Tahoe.

Website: www.getgoverned.com

Email: morgan@getgoverned.com

LinkedIn: https://www.linkedin.com/in/morgantemplar

NOTES:

Made in the USA
Middletown, DE
14 April 2019